Roman
MYTHOLOGY

Other titles in the *World Mythology* series include:

Roman
MYTHOLOGY

Don Nardo

ReferencePoint Press

San Diego, CA

© 2021 ReferencePoint Press, Inc.
Printed in the United States

For more information, contact:
ReferencePoint Press, Inc.
PO Box 27779
San Diego, CA 92198
www.ReferencePointPress.com

LIBRARY OF CONGRESS CATALOGING-IN-PUBLICATION DATA

Names: Nardo, Don, 1947- author.
Title: Roman mythology / by Don Nardo.
Description: San Diego, CA : ReferencePoint Press, 2020. | Series: World
    mythology series | Includes bibliographical references and index.
Identifiers: LCCN 2019049029 (print) | LCCN 2019049030 (ebook) | ISBN
    9781682828175 (library binding) | ISBN 9781682828182 (ebook)
Subjects: LCSH: Mythology, Roman--Juvenile literature. |
    Rome--Religion--Juvenile literature.
Classification: LCC BL803 .N37 2020 (print) | LCC BL803 (ebook) | DDC
    292.1/30937--dc23
LC record available at https://lccn.loc.gov/2019049029
LC ebook record available at https://lccn.loc.gov/2019049030

CONTENTS

LINEAGE OF ROME'S SEMI-DIVINE FOUNDERS

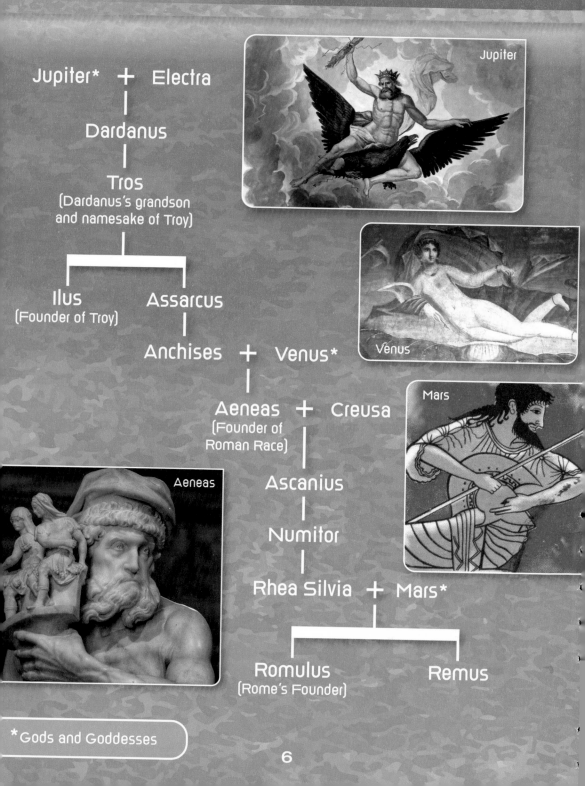

Jupiter* + Electra

Dardanus

Tros
(Dardanus's grandson
and namesake of Troy)

Ilus
(Founder of Troy)

Assarcus

Anchises + Venus*

Aeneas + Creusa
(Founder of
Roman Race)

Ascanius

Numitor

Rhea Silvia + Mars*

Romulus
(Rome's Founder)

Remus

Jupiter

Venus

Mars

Aeneas

*Gods and Goddesses

6

Blurring the Boundary Between Legend and Reality

The words *ancient Rome* often conjure up in the mind a sprawling city filled with majestic marble temples, bridges, statues, and the famed Colosseum. Within that city of 1 million inhabitants resided wealthy nobles, toga-clad senators, productive tradespeople, and disciplined professional soldiers. That was indeed the Rome of twenty centuries ago in the period historians call the early Roman Empire.

Five or six centuries before the beginnings of the Empire, however, Rome was a very different place. Still a dingy little farming community, it had no paved roads, and most citizens still lived in wooden huts with thatched roofs. Moreover, the culturally backward Romans were surrounded by formidable enemies, including Etruscans, Sabines, and others who sought to defeat and absorb them. Yet despite all the niceties they lacked, the early Romans were proud of their little nation-state beside the fast-moving Tiber River, and they were fiercely loyal to their homeland. That much is clear to anyone familiar with the myths of early Rome.

Reckless Courage

Typical of those tales is the one in which, in the late 500s BCE, a powerful army commanded by the Etruscan king Lars Porsenna marched on Rome, bent on conquering it and absorbing its farmlands. Hearing that the enemy was approaching, thousands of Roman farmers fled their fields. They sought the safety of the community's small urban center, erected on seven low hills near the Tiber.

In those days only a single large bridge—the Sublician—spanned the river and gave easy access to the urban center. A group of Roman farmers, who doubled as soldiers in such emergencies, helped the last civilians cross the bridge. These fighters, including the stalwart Horatius Cocles, then decided that they needed to chop down the structure's main supports, causing it to collapse. That way, the advancing Etruscans would not be able to enter the city proper.

There was little time left before the enemy's arrival. So Horatius told the others to start chopping. He alone, he said, would protect the bridge's entrance. Awed by this display of daring, they did as he suggested, while he blocked the path of the onrushing Etruscans. The great first-century-BCE Roman historian Livy would later call Horatius the steadfast individual "whom the fortune of Rome gave to be her shield on that day of peril."[1]

Mere minutes later, as Livy wrote, the enemy fighters "paused in sheer astonishment at such reckless courage." How, they wondered, could only one man hope to repel thousands? They soon received their answer. Horatius first said a little prayer to one of the local ancient gods, Father Tiber (who it was thought personified the river itself). The man asked that deity "to bless him and his sword." Perhaps, Horatius may have hoped, that would momentarily give him the godlike strength he would need to save the city. Then he proceeded to challenge "one after another to single combat, and mocking them." At the top of his voice, he called them slaves and accused them of caring not for "their own liberty," since they "were coming to destroy the liberty of others."[2]

Sheer amazement gripped the attackers as fearless Horatius engaged them one by one in single combat and slew more than ten of the finest champions Lars Porsenna could muster. The king's next move would have been to order fifty men to assault the Roman simultaneously. But it was too late. By this time the other Romans had broken the bridge's last support, and the structure abruptly tumbled into the river. Horatius fell along with it but managed to survive. He had saved the city.

Or at least this is what this famous Roman myth *claimed* that Horatius did. In truth, the later Romans could not be sure whether Horatius Cocles had even existed; and if he had, there was no proof that he had accomplished the clearly superhuman feat the legend ascribed to him. But this was the kind of myth the Romans most cherished and perpetuated—one in which a valiant

Sixteenth-century Italian artist Tommaso Laureti produced this painting showing the famous Roman hero Horatius Cocles defending the bridge across the Tiber River against the invading Etruscans led by King Lars Porsenna.

Roman warrior of old rose to the occasion and either saved the day or set an example of bravery and honor for later generations of Romans to follow. Also, as in most Roman myths, the gods played mainly background roles, such as revealing that Rome and its heroes had a grand destiny or perhaps instilling in those heroes some added courage and strength.

Fascinated by Beginnings

Thus, Horatius's stirring story illustrates that the main source of material for the Romans' myths was an imagined, legendary early history of their race, city, and country. The historical tales they perpetuated and respected were generally of two types. One consisted of foundation stories. In fact, the Romans were almost obsessed with tales about how various aspects of their civilization were established in the dim past. These included the origin of the Roman people, the founding of the city of Rome, the conduct of the first public sacrifices to the gods, the establishment of the early kingship, and so forth. As former University of Reading historian Jane F. Gardner tells it, during the reign of their first emperor, Augustus (30 BCE–14 CE), the Romans were captivated by "aetiology, that is, accounting for beginnings: the beginning of rituals, of place-names, of institutions, of cities, of the whole Roman people and its history."[3]

The principal reason the Romans of Livy's era so tightly embraced these foundation myths was that doing so fulfilled a crucial need. Such stories established their identity as a people. "We see the Romans defining themselves," Gardner writes, "through the stories they tell about their past, that is, though their myths."[4]

The other type of legendary historical tale dominating Roman mythology features heroes who were thought to have defended or saved Rome from hostile forces. Some were military officers and other upper-class individuals from noble families. But a number of them were simple farmers and other ordinary individuals, like Horatius, who rose to the occasion under extraordinary circumstances. Meanwhile, supporting these heroes' endeavors were the gods, led by mighty Jupiter. For the Romans, he boldly stated, he saw "no measure nor date, and I grant them dominion without end . . . the master race, the wearers of the toga. So it is willed!"[5]

Often, historians like Livy transmitted these tales of heroes and gods in story-like narratives rather than poetic verses. That conveyed the impression that such characters and events were truly historical and real rather than legendary. As Lincoln College scholar Donald L. Wasson explains it, "Whereas much of Greek mythology was transmitted through their poetry and drama, [most] Roman myths were written in prose, providing a sense of history." In Roman mythology, he adds, "the difference between history and myth was almost indistinguishable." Indeed, most Roman myths blur the boundary between legend and reality. Put bluntly, those old tales gave the Romans a distinct past. It was one that, in spite of being mostly mythical, instilled in them "a sense of national pride, an understanding of valor and honor, and insight into their destiny,"[6] says Wasson.

JUPITER
The chief Roman god

CHAPTER ONE

The Ancient Romans and Their Gods

Juno, wife of the chief Roman god, Jupiter, helped him protect Rome, which is often called the Eternal City. Yet in a myth created by the first-century-BCE Roman epic poet Virgil in his immortal *Aeneid*, she had not always favored the Romans. In fact, she had even tried to keep Rome from being established in the first place. This was because she hated the Trojans, the residents of the ancient city of Troy (in modern-day Turkey), and because Aeneas, who was destined to sail to Italy and there found the Roman race, was born a Trojan. So crafty and powerful Juno went to the god of the winds, Aeolus, and told him to brew up a storm to sink Aeneas's ships as he made the journey west. In Virgil's words, the winds "swirled out and swept the land in a hurricane." Soon, darkness descended "on the deep, thunder shackled the poles [masts], and the air crackled with fire. Everywhere death was at the sailor's elbow, terror played fast and loose with Aeneas's limbs, and he moaned and lifted his arms to the stars in prayer."[7]

Despite Juno's interference, Aeneas made it to Italy and fulfilled his destiny. Rome rose to greatness, and Juno came to admire him for it. The moral backing and other aid that various deities provided for Roman heroes was a common theme in Virgil's writings, as well as those of his equally famous literary colleagues,

Livy and Ovid. These writers all lived in an age when Rome was already the strongest nation-state in the known world. They and other highly educated Romans sought to show how and why Rome had risen to such lofty status. To some degree, they declared, it was because the gods and fate had long ago decreed that the Romans were the chosen people, destined to rule all humanity forever. In this way, the *Aeneid* and other masterworks of the age either created or reinforced a mythology whose main characters and events were depicted as part of Rome's legendary history.

Myth vs. Reality and the Gods' Roles

The degree to which Rome's legendary narrative and real history coincided may never be known for certain. Modern archaeologists and historians are constantly uncovering new evidence that expands or tweaks what is already known about that history. One thing is certain, however. The bulk of Roman mythology revolves around that early legendary history. A clear example is that Livy, Virgil, and other first-century-BCE Roman writers and scholars completely accepted and expanded the city's official foundation myth. In it, an early shepherd with royal blood—Romulus—established Rome in 753 BCE on a formerly uninhabited spot beside the Tiber River. Romulus may not have been a real person, and Rome was likely not actually established during that century. But the later Romans staunchly believed he was their real founder and accepted that founding date. So those concepts remained central in their mythology.

MARS
The Roman version of Ares, the Greek god of war

It should be noted that a god plays a role in Romulus's story as told by Livy and his contemporaries. Namely, they claimed that Mars, god of war, got a Roman priestess name Rhea Silvia pregnant, and nine months later she gave birth to Romulus and his brother, Remus. That Mars would appear in this tale, much as

Juno appears in Virgil's *Aeneid*, is not surprising. After all, the Romans believed strongly in the existence of powerful divine beings who could, at will, intervene in human affairs. Because of these beliefs, like the Greeks and other ancient peoples, the Romans of Livy's and Virgil's day erected temples to honor Mars, Juno, Jupiter, and other gods. They also regularly worshipped those deities by praying and making offerings to them and held elaborate annual religious festivals for them.

Nevertheless, when the Romans began recording their myths in a serious way via the pens of Virgil, Livy, and their contemporaries, the gods usually played fairly small roles in those stories. Juno's urging the wind god to sink Aeneas's ships and Mars's affair with the priestess are among the chief examples. Another

This illustration from a fifteenth-century Italian book shows masons, woodworkers, and other builders laboring to create the new city of Rome. The city's founder, Romulus, and his brother Remus inspect the construction site at lower right.

is how the Roman goddess of love, Venus, makes Dido, queen of the North African city of Carthage, fall in love with Aeneas but does little else in the story. These and other minor deeds of deities in the *Aeneid* were mostly Virgil's own inventions. In fact, before that long poem was written in the first century BCE, Juno and the other Roman deities had few or no myths.

One principal reason for this dearth of early Roman stories about the gods is the way the Romans initially saw the deities they worshipped. Before the Roman people came into close contact with the Greek city-states and kingdoms in the last four centuries BCE, they worshipped a group of deities called *numina*. Regarding religious beliefs, the Romans saw those entities as very simplistic and largely formless nature spirits. Each had one or two mainly small-scale functions and influenced only a small, localized aspect of life. Janus, god of doorways, was an example. (Because people come and go via doorways, he was also the deity of beginnings and endings.) As the late, great historian R.M. Ogilvie pointed out:

JANUS
An early Roman god thought to watch over doorways

> Most of the things which were vital for the well-being of society were thought of as functions of a god or as gods functioning. A house is only as secure as its door. The opening and closing of the door, and the passage of a person from the privacy of the home into the racket of the outside world, and *vice versa*, can be critical events, and, in consequence, they were held to be in the power of a god: Janus.[8]

Similarly, the *numen* (singular of *numina*) called Sylvanus protected woodcutters, and another, Concordia, oversaw agreements and contracts. Terminus oversaw boundaries, Flora made flowers grow, Robigus caused mildew to form, and an early version of Jupiter controlled the sky and thunder. There were hundreds of other numina, many of them the bodiless spirits of people's ancestors.

It must be stressed that these so-called gods were nothing like the Greek deities. The numina lacked bodies and personalities and in substance were little more than mere names and concepts. Indeed, Jane F. Gardner says, they also had no myths to speak of because they "lacked personal adventures and family relationships."[9] Thus, people did not compile and retell tales about these spirits, as the Greeks did about their own gods.

Moreover, no early Roman believed the numina were powerful enough to have created the universe, so the early Romans had no story that told how the world came to be. Nor did the early Romans erect temples or statues for the invisible spirits they worshipped. That worship consisted of saying prayers and making simple offerings either in the home or outside in a field. This rudimentary vision of simplistic spiritual forces, with its lack of an accompanying mythology, was a major reason why the Romans based most of their myths on human leaders and heroes of the dim past.

Enter the Greeks

By contrast, the major Greek gods looked and acted like humans and had both colorful personalities and substantial powers, including the ability to create both the world and humanity. Those deities were also characters in large numbers of complex, equally colorful myths. In addition, the Greeks celebrated their gods and myths through paintings, sculptures, temple architecture, and other artistic works that were nothing less than magnificent in scope and execution.

Although over time the Romans invaded and conquered the Greek lands, it was plain to most Romans that Greek religion and artistic culture were superior to their Roman counterparts. During those invasions, the Romans did not want to appear to be uncultured country bumpkins beside those they had conquered.

Virgil Involves the Gods in His Famous Hero Tale

In his great epic the *Aeneid*, Virgil tells about the Trojan hero Aeneas's journey to Italy, where he eventually establishes a line of rulers who will, over the course of time, lead to Romulus, Rome's founder. Although this tale, arguably the greatest single Roman myth, is mainly an adventure story about human heroes and villains, Virgil carefully inserted divine beings into the narrative—most notably Juno, wife of Jupiter. She at first favors Carthage and therefore wants to stop Aeneas from founding the Roman race. In one of her failed attempts to thwart his mission, she orders her divine messenger, Iris, to incite the Trojan women to burn Aeneas's ships while they are temporarily beached in Sicily. Seeing the rising smoke, Aeneas and the other men try to put out the blazes. "The creeping fires fastened upon the keels," Virgil wrote, "and the danger threatened every part of the ships. Though every hero slaved with all his might, and they poured in floods of water, they made no headway." Desperate, Aeneas prayed to mighty Jupiter for help. "Grant our fleet to escape from the flames!" Aeneas cried out. Hardly had the words escaped his mouth when darkness descended on the beaches and an enormous rainstorm struck. "The whole sky opened in a blinding cloudburst," Virgil continued. It was plain to Aeneas that Jupiter's intervention, which saved the fleet, was indication that the strongest of the gods was on his side and his mission would likely succeed.

Virgil, *Aeneid*, trans. Patric Dickinson. New York: New American Library, 2002, p. 137.

Therefore, even as they exerted political control over the Greeks, the Romans consciously absorbed and emulated many aspects of Greek religion and art.

The first aspect of Greek religion the Romans borrowed was the way the Greeks envisioned their gods—as full-fledged beings who looked like people but were vastly more powerful than any humans. The Romans began to associate some of their simplistic numina with the much more complex Greek deities. For instance, Jupiter, originally a sky spirit with rather limited abilities, underwent a major makeover into the equivalent of the Greek Zeus. The latter was not only in charge of the sky and lightning but was also the supreme leader of the entire Greek pantheon and thereby the overlord of the universe. The Romans took advantage of the fact that they had long worshipped a sky spirit in charge of lightning and claimed that he—Jupiter—was their version of Zeus.

In a similar manner, Mars had been a simple Roman numen who oversaw certain aspects of farmers' fields. That role included defending those fields if necessary, making it possible to interpret him as a military figure, so he was a natural choice to become the Roman equivalent of Ares, the Greek god of war. In a like manner, Ceres, a Roman deity who helped make plants grow, became associated with Demeter, the Greek goddess of agriculture.

A few other examples of such associations of Roman deities with Greeks ones included Juno, the Roman version of Zeus's wife, Hera; Vulcan, the Roman equivalent of Hephaestus, the Greek god of forges; and Faunus, the Roman version of the Greek

Faunus, pictured in this sixteenth-century painting, was the Roman version of Pan, the Greek god of flocks and shepherds. The great Roman poet Virgil claimed that in addition to his divine duties, Faunus served as a very early legendary king of the Latin tribes.

Livy the Myth Teller

Titus Livius, popularly known as Livy, was the leading historian and prose writer of Rome's Augustan Age of literature, spanning the late first century BCE and early first century CE. Born in 59 BCE in Patavium (today called Padua), in northern Italy, he spent most of his years in Rome. There he composed his grand masterwork, the *Ab urbe condita libri* (in English, the *History of Rome from Its Foundation*). Of its original 142 volumes, only 35 have survived—books 1–10, 21–45, and a small portion of 91. The first several books are a treasure trove from a mythological standpoint because they contain Livy's detailed tellings of key foundation and heroic myths. Covered are Rome's "father" and founder, Romulus; the last king, Tarquin the Proud; the valiant Horatii brothers; Horatius Cocles, who famously defended the bridge against an Etruscan army; and Brutus, Cloelia, Coriolanus, Cincinnatus, and other early Roman heroic figures. It must be noted that Livy was not a skilled historian. The sources he employed varied widely in accuracy and writing quality, and he paid little attention to economic and social history. Yet strictly as a myth teller he was highly effective. The late literary scholar J. Wight Duff pointed out that Livy possessed a "gift of reverence for the majesty of Rome, [and] the gift of enthusiasm for olden times, olden heroes, and olden virtues." Moreover, his enormous masterwork "is unsurpassed in its fidelity [faithfulness] to Rome's national character."

J. Wight Duff, *A Literary History of Rome, from the Origins to the Close of the Golden Age.* New York: Barnes & Noble, 1963, pp. 473–74.

god of flocks and shepherds, Pan. Overall, as Ogilvie writes, the Greeks supplied the Romans with "ideas about their own gods, so that it is difficult to speak about 'Roman' religion as a separate thing. Roman religion is essentially the result of the fusion of primitive [Roman] and Greek elements."[10]

Inventing New Myths

That profound influence of Greek religion on Roman beliefs is proved by the fact that the Romans were not content merely to borrow the physical images and duties of the Greek gods. Roman civilization absorbed all sorts of other religious elements from the

Greeks as well. A prime example was building large-scale temples to honor the gods. In addition, the Romans increasingly produced paintings, mosaics, statues, and other artistic renderings of those heavenly beings.

Also, because the original Roman deities had lacked myths of their own, the Romans absorbed the numerous colorful tales connected to the Greek gods. For example, most of the myths associated with Zeus became part of Jupiter's personal biography. Zeus's daughter Athena, goddess of wisdom, had sprung fully grown from his head, and therefore so did Athena's Roman equivalent—Minerva—emerge from Jupiter's head.

Despite this wholesale borrowing of myths from the Greeks, the Romans could not hide the fact that these were originally Greek stories. Even when the first-century-BCE Roman poet Ovid compiled his famous retellings of important myths—the *Metamorphoses*—he clearly separated the Greek ones from the Roman ones. First, he retold many of the principal Greek myths, giving the gods their Roman names. He then told a set of newer Roman myths; true to form, those tales mostly recount the heroic, partly fictional early history that the Romans of his day thought had taken place.

A large proportion of these Roman tales were new myths introduced by Ovid and his colleagues Livy, Virgil, and the other Augustan writers. They lived in the so-called Augustan Age of Roman literature (ca. 43 BCE–ca. 18 CE), named for their ruler, the first Roman emperor, Augustus. An astute individual and skilled ruler, he recognized that a vital key to justifying Rome's destiny to rule the world was to give Rome a mythology as comprehensive and compelling as that of the Greeks. To this end, he encouraged the gifted writers of his day to flesh out the few existing legends of Rome's founding and rise to greatness.

Those writers fulfilled that mission with great skill and success. As Gardner says, the Augustan authors "depicted Rome itself and its people as marked out by the gods to be the destined rulers of the whole world."[11] Moreover, several of those writers

Minerva, pictured in this early modern European painting, was the Roman goddess of wisdom. From roughly the second century BCE on, the Romans equated her with the Greek goddess Athena.

not only glorified Rome by telling its mythical history, they even injected Augustus's adoptive father, Julius Caesar, and Augustus himself into the new myths. Ovid ended the *Metamorphoses*, for example, by recalling Caesar's 44 BCE assassination and depicting the gods leading the fallen "hero" upward into heaven and making him one of their number. Furthermore, Ovid wrote, "Augustus, leaving the world he rules, will make his way to heaven"[12] and there become divine.

Virgil did something similar in the *Aeneid* by working references to Augustus into supposedly ancient mythical events that Virgil had largely invented. In the narrative, the hero Aeneas visits his deceased father, Anchises, in the underworld. The older man's spirit reveals a glorious future for Rome, including the ultimate emergence of Augustus: "Here is the very man whom you have heard so often promised you [in prophecy], Augustus Caesar, your child of the Divine who shall refound a golden age for [Rome]."[13]

Thrilling and Inspiring Later Generations

Meanwhile, Livy and other Augustan writers expanded a few existing legendary figures and events into a complex new mythical story of early Rome, making it sound like actual history. In so doing, they introduced new myths about the gods, intending to make up for the scarcity of original, non-Greek stories about those deities. A clear example is the way Livy connected Jupiter to Numa Pompilius, Rome's second early king and himself a mythical figure. In Livy's tale, King Numa wanted to obtain Jupiter's advice on what the future of the Roman nation and people would be. But he did not know how to contact that mighty god. So the king sought out a minor deity—Faunus, god of flocks and shepherds. (Faunus had originated as a simple numen; later, thanks to Greek influence on Roman religion, he became a full-bodied divine being.) Numa got Faunus drunk in hopes that it would make him more willing to answer questions. This plan worked because when Numa said he desired to summon Jupiter to earth, Faunus revealed how to go about it.

Soon the king of the gods arrived and conferred with Numa. They discussed various matters, including Rome's destiny. Jupiter said that the next day he would send signs showing that Rome was fated to rule humanity forever. True to his word, the following day the god hurled three huge lightning bolts across a clear sky and then tossed down a magnificent shield symbolizing Rome's great destiny.

In the same way, the Augustan writers made Mars the father of Romulus, Rome's founder. They also coined myths in which Mars had an affair with the love goddess, Venus. The purpose of this myth was to connect Romulus's establishment of Rome with the founding of the Roman race by Aeneas. In the new mythology Venus was Aeneas's mother. Thus, Venus had mated with the fathers of both of Rome's principal founders, thereby linking them.

Perhaps at no other time in history did a handful of writers boldly create a new set of national myths in so short a time as Virgil, Livy, and their colleagues did. After Roman religion had been overshadowed for so long by the Greeks and their myths, these writers firmly established a uniquely Roman mythology. With its tales of Roman founders, leaders, and heroes of old, all guided by divine hands, it has thrilled and inspired generation after generation of writers and readers right up to the present day.

CHAPTER TWO

Rome's Primary Foundation Myths

"Come, dear guest," says Dido, queen of the North African kingdom of Carthage, "tell us the whole tale from the beginning." Her guest at a lavish royal supper is the strapping young warrior Aeneas, who has recently landed in Carthage. A Trojan prince, he and his close followers had fled when the Greeks sacked his native city of Troy and had begun wandering the seas in search of a new home. Dido bids him to describe "the cunning of the Greeks, your country's ruin, and your wanderings."[14]

Aeneas answers the queen and in so doing initiates the main narrative of Virgil's mighty epic, the *Aeneid*. In the ensuing story, the young man tells of his wanderings, as Dido requested. Then he leaves Carthage and sails to Italy, where he becomes the father of a new and noble race of people—the Romans.

This connection between the most famous of all Greek myths—that of the Trojan War—and the founding of the Roman people was no accident. It was instead the result of Virgil's and other Augustan Roman writers' attempts to make Rome's beginnings seem as lofty and respectable as possible. After all, Roman intellectuals understood that they lacked the esteemed literary tradition the Greeks enjoyed. The seventh-century-BCE Greek bard Homer's glorious epics, the *Iliad* and the *Odyssey*, were renowned throughout the known world; the Romans had nothing like them before Virgil's time, and his *Aeneid* was an attempt to boost the stature of Rome's history and heroes.

DIDO
The queen of Carthage who falls in love with Aeneas

In the first century BCE, when Augustus was establishing a bold new Roman order, describing the foundation of the Roman race itself seemed only natural. While Virgil approached that task with eagerness and vigor, his colleague Livy did the same regarding another key foundation myth. In his massive history of Rome, Livy devoted much space to the story of one of Aeneas's supposed descendants—Romulus. In Rome's heroic folklore, Romulus laid the first stones of the city destined to rule the known world and served as its first king.

The tales of Aeneas and Romulus, Jane F. Gardner points out, "enabled the Romans to claim their own place in the tradition that was regarded as in a sense 'historical' [and part] of the Greek heroic past."[15] Noted scholar T.J. Cornell agrees. These key Roman myths gave the Romans "a respect-

ROMULUS
A descendant of Aeneas and the founder of the city of Rome

able identity in the eyes of a wider world," he says, "and one that could be used to advantage in their dealings with the Greeks."[16]

Beware of Greeks Bearing Gifts!

In fact, as Virgil told it, the Trojans, like the later Romans, were easily the equal of the Greeks in various ways, including war. After besieging Troy for ten long years, he explained in the *Aeneid*, the Greeks were unable to take the city solely through manly fighting. So they resorted to despicable trickery. They built a huge, hollow wooden horse, hid some soldiers inside, left it on the plain before Troy, and pretended to give up the war. When the Greek ships sailed away, however, they did not return to Greece but instead hid in a nearby cove. They hoped the Trojans would drag the

The famous Trojan Horse, seen here, was hollow and when the Trojans dragged it into their city, they did not realize that Greek soldiers were hiding inside. Homer did not mention the horse in his Iliad but did describe it in his other epic, the Odyssey, as did Virgil in his Aeneid.

horse into the city, where the hidden warriors could sneak out in the dead of night and open the gates to the returning Greeks.

The plan might have failed if the Trojans had listened to one of their priests, who warned his countrymen not to trust the Greeks. He worriedly exclaimed (according Virgil), "Either the Greeks have hidden some men inside this wooden monster, or in itself it is a foul contrivance [built] for overthrowing our walls . . . or there is some other trick in it. Whatever it be, I am nothing but apprehensive of the motives of the Greeks, even as givers of gifts."[17] (The priest's warning is the source of the common adage "Beware of Greeks bearing gifts.")

Unfortunately for the Trojans, they did not take the priest's advice to burn the giant horse. They dragged it into the city, and sure enough, that night Troy fell to the Greeks. Almost all the inhabitants were either killed or forced into slavery. An exception was a small band of locals led by Aeneas, the son of Anchises, a cousin of Troy's king. Aeneas and his followers managed to escape the burning city and sailed out into the Aegean Sea.

The Mysterious Prediction

In the years that followed, the Trojan exiles wandered through unfamiliar regions. All the while a handful of gods watched them from somewhere high above. Jupiter, the chief deity, wanted Aeneas to make it to Italy and thereby fulfill a prophecy that Rome would someday rise and rule the world. So from time to time he helped the Trojan band. A dramatic example was when he sent a massive rainstorm to put out a fire that threatened to destroy Aeneas's vessels. Meanwhile, Jupiter's divine wife—Juno—desired that the Trojans *not* make it to Italy because she wanted her favorite city, Carthage, to eventually rule the world. For that reason, she attempted, unsuccessfully, to thwart the travelers' progress. It was she, for instance, who brought about the fire that Jupiter extinguished.

Eventually, the progress that Juno failed to impede brought Aeneas and his followers to Carthage, where they met Queen Dido. Thanks to a spell cast over her by the love goddess, Venus, Dido fell deeply in love with the handsome young Aeneas and was hurt and angered when he decided to leave and head for Italy. He was determined to get there, because after escaping Troy, he had heard a mysterious prediction from none other than the god of prophecy, Apollo. Part of the divine message had stated, "There is a place

APOLLO
The god of prophecy, who tells Aeneas that he should sail to Italy

the Greeks have called Hesperia, the western land." The people who dwell there call themselves "Italians, after Italus, one of their leaders. There lies your true home."[18]

Convinced that the gods had willed him and his followers to end up in Italy, Aeneas journeyed there. The first landfall was at Cumae, on the peninsula's southwestern shore. There the Trojan encountered the Sibyl, a shadowy woman wearing a black robe who it was said could foresee future events. She went into a trance and told him about Latium. A wonderfully fertile plain lying many miles north of Cumae, it was, she said, where he should establish a new kingdom.

The Sibyl did the stranger another favor. She led him down a winding secret path to the outer edge of the dark underworld. There the man came upon the spirit of his father, Anchises, who had died during the group's wanderings. The older man provided his son with a glimpse of the future of the noble race Aeneas would soon create. "I shall show you the whole span of our destiny," Anchises remarked. In lovely Latium, Aeneas's children would erect the fair city of Alba Longa; moreover, the subsequent line of Alban rulers would eventually lead to a man who would found another new city—Rome. That heroic individual would be called Romulus. Anchises added proudly, "Our glorious Rome shall rule the whole wide world, and her spirit shall match the spirit of the gods."[19]

After bidding his father's spirit farewell, Aeneas collected his followers and sailed northward toward Latium. Reaching that region, the wayward Trojan met the local ruler and fell in love with his daughter, Lavinia. The problem was that another local nobleman, Turnus, had already proposed to her. At this point Juno made one more try at ruining Aeneas. She sent the flying spirit of anger—Alecto—to stir up hatred and war between the Trojans and local Latins. As a result, Aeneas and Turnus engaged in a

This enamel, based on an earlier woodcut, shows Juno, seated on a golden throne, and ordering the flying spirit Alecto to stir up trouble between the Trojans and local Italians.

fearsome fight to the death for the hand of Lavinia. In the words of modern myth teller Norma L. Goodrich, "Like two bulls they met, Aeneas and Turnus, horn to horn and shield to shield, struggling for footing, swords flashing and then locked to the hilt, forehead to forehead."[20]

Aeneas won the battle and soon afterward married Lavinia. Together they established a city—called Lavinium after her. In so doing, they merged the Trojan and Latin races, thereby giving rise to a new and supremely noble race—the Romans. Great Jupiter himself declared that their empire would someday span the universe and "the bitter centuries of war shall cease then, [and] the world grow mild at last."[21]

One Founder Enough?

When comparing the myth in which Romulus and Remus together establish Rome to the one in which Romulus founded Rome alone, a few modern scholars have tried to figure out where the character Remus came from. As noted scholar of ancient Roman myths Jane F. Gardner puts it, Romulus was unquestionably Rome's founder, so "when and why did he acquire a twin? One founder is enough!" Attempting to answer this question, Gardner and other experts on Roman mythology point to evidence showing that back in the 500s BCE, Greek myth tellers began mentioning a figure named Romus. Apparently, he was a generic sort of city founder who established numerous towns. Soon the early Romans heard about him and adopted him, calling him Romulus. Yet the Greeks who had cities in Italy at that time argued that Romulus and Romus were distinctly different characters. This prompted the introduction of a new myth in which the two were twin brothers, and the early Romans eagerly accepted that idea. Perhaps because the names Romulus and Romus sounded too much alike, they changed Romus to Remus. That was the version that later Roman historians, including Livy, perpetuated. In whatever manner the most popular version of the myth may have developed, by the first century BCE average Romans spoke about Romulus with the same awed and reverent tone that modern Americans use when speaking about George Washington and the other US founding fathers.

Jane F. Gardner, *Roman Myths.* Austin: University of Texas Press, 1993, p. 31.

An Excellent Location for a City

So ended the grand story of Aeneas, as told by Virgil and other Augustan Roman writers. Virgil had briefly mentioned one of Aeneas's descendants, Romulus, in Anchises's speech about Rome's glorious future. But Virgil allowed other writers to fill in the details about that other prominent Roman founder. In addition to Livy's fulsome account of Rome's founding by Romulus, there was a detailed biography of Romulus by the first-century-CE Greek writer Plutarch.

Thanks to Livy and Plutarch, therefore, every Roman from their era onward had almost intimate knowledge of Rome's founder

and first king. The most popular tales described Romulus's mirac-
ulous survival as a baby, along with his twin brother, Remus. Supposedly, they were grandchildren of Numitor, a king of Alba Longa
and a direct descendant of Aeneas. Not long after the twins' birth,
the story goes, Numitor's brother usurped Alba's throne and ordered the infants to be drowned in the Tiber River. Luckily for the
children, however, they drifted to shore, and a female wolf fed and
protected them. In time a local shepherd named Faustulus found
the twin boys and raised them. They quickly grew to become
physically strong and emotionally mature. This was especially true
of Romulus, who in Plutarch's words displayed the wisdom "of a
statesman, and in all his dealings with their neighbors, whether
relating to feeding of flocks or to hunting, gave the idea of being
born rather to rule than to obey."[22]

Somehow Faustulus found out that his adopted sons were
the grandsons of the rightful monarch, Numitor. When he felt the
time was right, the shepherd revealed that information to Romulus and Remus, who became determined to restore Numitor to
his throne. They gathered some faithful followers and ousted the
usurper. Soon afterward, as Livy recounted, the twin brothers
"saluted their grandfather as the [lawful] king."[23]

Having restored order in Alba Longa, Romulus and his
brother decided to create a new city of their own. They traveled to the northern edge of the fertile Latium plain and found
a spot where a cluster of low hills rose near a bend in the Tiber
River. It appeared to be an excellent location for a city because
it bordered both much rich farmland and a river that led out
to the open sea. In picking this location, the young men may
have been secretly aided by a god—great Jupiter himself. Unknown to the brothers, that deity had been watching their progress with much interest because he strongly desired that Rome
should be established.

Jupiter saw that Romulus and Remus had long maintained
friendly relations with each other, so the god was saddened

when one day the brothers started arguing hotly about some minor matter. A scuffle ensued, and in the heat of the action Romulus killed Remus. That left Romulus alone, aided by his closest friends and followers, to establish the new town.

According to Plutarch, Romulus "sent for men out of Tuscany," the region lying directly to the north, where an advanced Italian people, the Etruscans, dwelled in small cities of their own. These carpenters, masons, priests, and other experts on urban living "directed him by sacred usages and written rules in all the ceremonies to be observed." Then the founder "fitted to a plough a [bronze] ploughshare, and, yoking together a bull and a cow, drove himself a deep line or furrow round the bounds." In this way he marked where the city's outer walls and main gate would rise. Plutarch continued, "It is universally agreed to have been the twenty-first of April, and that day the Romans annually keep holy, calling it their country's birthday."[24]

The Sabine Women

Romulus realized that his roughly one hundred followers were not enough people to populate a strong and important new city. Thus, as Livy told it, hoping to "fill up his big new town, he [made it] a place of asylum for fugitives. Here fled for refuge all the [outcasts] from the neighboring peoples, some free, some slaves, and all of them wanting nothing more than a fresh start.[25]

Although this approach did bring many settlers to the infant Rome, Romulus was disappointed that nearly all of them were men. It was plain to see that the city could not keep expanding unless many of the male citizens could find brides and establish families. To this end, the founder hatched a bold plan. He sent word to the residents of all the nearby towns that the Romans were going to have a large-scale religious festival that would include food, entertainment, and athletic contests.

Many of those who showed up for the festival were female members of a Latin-speaking people known as the Sabines. Little did they realize what Romulus had planned for them. At

This oil painting by the eighteenth-century artist Jacques-Louis David shows the mythical moment when the Sabine women step out between the Roman and Sabine armies and plead for peace between the two peoples.

a signal given at the height of the celebration, each of Romulus's male followers suddenly grabbed hold of a young, unmarried Sabine woman and dragged her away to his house. The girls' parents and siblings hurried back to their villages and described the incident. Romulus sent messengers to these towns to assure the Sabines that the young women would be treated well. Indeed, he said, they would become respectable Roman wives.

The angry Sabine leaders ignored these words and sent an army to retrieve the girls by force. Several small skirmishes between Roman and Sabine soldiers eventually led up to some battles within Rome itself. In one a group of Sabines tried to pass through a gate leading to some of the forums, or town squares. As Ovid told it, Janus, the god who oversaw doorways, including gates, decided to intervene by turning some of the town's water supply against the enemy. The deity himself supposedly later recounted what he did, saying, "By the power I wield, I opened the fountains' mouths and spouted out a sudden gush of water; but

Virgil the Myth Teller

Virgil was the shortened and widely popular name for the first-century-BCE Roman writer Publius Vergilius Maro. His great claim to fame was one of the finest and most influential of all ancient mythological works—the *Aeneid*. In 42 BCE, when he was almost thirty, he met the noted Roman literary patron Gaius Maecenas, who thereafter sponsored him. Through Maecenas, Virgil met the young Octavian, Julius Caesar's adopted son, who was destined to become Rome's first emperor under the name Augustus. The poet made a name for himself with the *Eclogues*, a collection of short poems about country life, and he followed that up with another set of similar verses, the *Georgics*. But the *Aeneid* was by far his greatest and most popular work. This long, masterful version of the myth of the founding of the Roman race by a Trojan prince instantly became Rome's national patriotic epic. In part this was because Virgil possessed the ability to make his readers feel a strong nostalgia for the "good old days." In the words of historian John B. Firth, the work is filled with a "spirit of humanity and religion." In fact, "deep religion and intense burning patriotism—in these lie the secret of Virgil's influence. And [they] were [inevitably] intertwined. He looked back with regret to the bygone days when men lived simpler lives, and not only feared, but walked with, the gods."

John B. Firth, *Augustus Caesar and the Organization of the Empire of Rome*. Sydney, Australia: Wentworth, 2016, pp. 208–09.

first I threw sulfur into the water channels, that the boiling liquid might bar the way against [the Sabines]."[26]

Although the god's act stopped one group of Sabines, a much larger one gathered in the town's center, where hundreds of Roman defenders waited. As the opposing fighters approached one another, however, they beheld an unexpected sight. The young women who had earlier been forced into marriage suddenly ran out and stood between the armies. They urged the soldiers on both sides to lay down their weapons. The women had come to accept the Roman men as their husbands, they said, and they did not want to see their fathers and new husbands killing one another. After that, a historic deal was struck. "Conditions were agreed upon," Plutarch wrote, that the women would "stay where they were [and] that the Romans and Sabines should inhabit the city together."[27]

This compelling foundation story appealed to the later Romans because it clearly demonstrated the traits that helped make Rome great. The tale establishes "the identity of the Roman people as a mixture of different ethnic groups," Cornell explains. As time went on, Rome would absorb numerous other regional and national groups. In this way, the Romans became a unique people who "built up their power by extending their citizenship and continuously admitting new elements into their midst."[28] The myth resonated so strongly with later generations of Romans because it seemed to confirm who they were as a people.

CHAPTER THREE

The Warrior Heroes of Early Rome

Like the Greeks in their own mythology, the Romans had myths featuring warrior heroes of olden times whom people in later generations looked back at with feelings of wonder and respect. There was a marked difference between the Greek and Roman mythical warriors, however. Most of the Greek ones were said to have lived in the distant past, in a magical era in which gods routinely descended to earth and interacted with humans. The classical Greeks called it the Age of Heroes and agreed that it took place many centuries before Greek civilization arose.

Most of the Roman heroes, by contrast, were warriors said to have lived in the period of Rome's Monarchy (ca. 753–ca. 509 BCE) and early Republic (ca. 509–ca. 350 BCE). That era did predate the Augustan Age, in which Virgil, Livy, and other Roman writers recorded the myths, but only by a few centuries. The stories of Rome's heroes, therefore, freely combined mythical occurrences with real historical events. Many of these legendary Roman heroes appeared, in retrospect, to have superhuman strength and morals. This was because one or more gods supposedly favored each hero and instilled in him those above-average abilities.

The deeds of the bygone warrior heroes were potent inspiration for manly conduct for later generations of Romans, who believed those champions were their immediate ancestors. "The noblest Roman families," Jane F. Gardner writes, "were particularly proud to include such stories in their family histories, and, at least during the Republic, continued for a long time to model their conduct upon them." Moreover, all Roman children were taught about "the legends of early history, which exemplified the virtues that the Romans liked to think were part of the essential Roman character, and stressed in particular the principle that the welfare of Rome must come before the desires of the individual, and even before loyalty to the family group."[29]

A Pity to Resort to Bloodshed?

Three renowned early patriots who were quick to put their country first came from one of Rome's richest and best-known families, the Horatii. Livy and other Augustan writers reckoned that the three Horatii brothers lived during the mid-600s BCE, when, according to legend, Tullus Hostilius was Rome's king.

During Tullus's reign, Rome went to war with the nearby city-state of Alba Longa. In the previous century that place had given rise to Rome's illustrious founder, Romulus, and the two towns had stayed on good terms for a while after Romulus had passed on. In recent years, however, men from each city had been raiding one another's cattle, which poisoned relations between the two peoples. Unable to maintain peace any more with Alba's ruler, Mettius Fufetius, King Tullus declared war on Alba Longa. Soon, according to Livy, "preparations on a grand scale were put in hand by both peoples for a struggle." In the days that followed, the Albans moved more quickly than the Romans, and a large Alban army "took up an entrenched position within Roman territory and not more than five miles from the town."[30]

The next day the Romans fielded their own army. Tullus and Mettius met one last time to try to strike a peace deal. After all,

THE HORATII
Three Roman brothers who famously fought three brothers from a rival city-state

both men acknowledged that the two peoples were related by blood and culture and that it would be a pity if they resorted to bloodshed. Mettius pleaded with Tullus to join with him in finding a better solution to their grievances.

A Fateful Clash

The two leaders did manage to make a deal. Instead of waging full-scale war, they would each pick three soldiers who would fight to the death. If the Roman combatants won, Alba Longa would have to submit to Roman rule. Similarly, if the Alban fighters were victorious, Rome would become submissive.

The three Roman soldiers chosen were the Horatii brothers. They faced off against three men from a no-less-noble Alban family—the Curiatii. On a mutually agreed-upon day, the members of the two armies

A seventeenth-century painting shows part of the legendary battle of the champions, which pitted the Horatii—three Roman brothers— against the Curiatii—three Alban brothers. Two of the Horatii were slain, but the third one defeated the Albans, giving Rome the victory.

stood by and watched as, at the blast of a trumpet, the six young men drew their weapons and began the fateful clash. Hearing the "clang of shield on shield," Livy wrote, "a thrill ran through the massed spectators, breathless and speechless while as yet neither side had the advantage. Soon the combatants were locked in a deadly grapple. Bodies writhed and twisted, the leaping blades parried and thrust, and blood began to flow."[31]

Minutes later, two of the Horatii lay dead, and their brother now faced the three Curiatii alone. The Roman onlookers were filled with despair, sure that their side was about to lose. To their surprise, however, the last of the Horatii proceeded to put on an incredible display of fighting skill and bravery that in their minds could only have been inspired in him by the gods. He managed to slay all three Albans, giving Rome the coveted victory. For their part, the Albans were sorely disappointed, but they lived up to their side of the agreement. Thereafter, Rome controlled and eventually absorbed Alba Longa.

> **GAIUS MUCIUS SCAEVOLA**
> A young patriot who thrust his hand into a fire to demonstrate his loyalty to Rome

The Wrong Man

The later Romans were thrilled to recite and perpetuate another exciting myth about a warrior of divinely inspired prowess. He was Gaius Mucius Scaevola, whose last name means "left-handed" in Latin. His story is set in the same period as the famous tale of brave Horatius's single-handed defense of the bridge. After Horatius and his companions chopped down the bridge, keeping the Etruscans from entering Rome, the Etruscan king, Lars Porsenna, was duly frustrated. But he refused to give up his attempt to conquer the Romans. In the months that followed, he brought in more soldiers plus siege equipment and tried to starve Rome into submission.

> **LARS PORSENNA**
> The Etruscan king whom Scaevola attempted to assassinate

The steadfast Roman hero Gaius Mucius Scaevola thrusts his hand into the fire as the enemy king, Lars Porsenna, looks on. The latter learned that three hundred more Roman men just as brave as Scaevola were ready to give up their lives in order to assassinate Porsenna.

The patriotic young Roman then known simply as Gaius Mucius, decided to try to strike a blow for his country. He went to the senators who controlled the government and described his daring plan. "I wish," he said, according to Livy's account, "to cross the river and to enter, if I can, the enemy's lines."[32] The youth went on to tell how he would use a sharp dagger to assassinate the Etruscan king.

The senators approved Mucius's scheme, and he proceeded to cross the river at night, managing to evade the Etruscan guards on the opposite bank. Livy told what happened when the young man entered the enemy camp:

> He took his stand, in the crowd, close to the raised platform where the king was sitting. A great many people were present, as it was pay-day for the army. By the side of the king sat his secretary, very busy. He was dressed much like his master, and [Mucius] could not be sure which was the secretary and which the king. . . . Mucius took a chance, and stabbed the secretary. There was a cry of alarm and he was seized by the guards.[33]

A Display of Raw Courage

After he was taken into custody, the young Roman displayed a defiant, fearless attitude toward his captors. Brought before Porsenna, he declared, "I am a Roman. My name is Gaius Mucius. I came here to kill you, my enemy. I have as much courage to die as to kill. It is our Roman way to do and to suffer bravely. Nor am I alone in my resolve against your life. Behind me is a long line of men eager for the same honor."[34]

Taken aback by this impudent outburst, the king threatened that he would have Mucius burned alive if he did not reveal more about those would-be assassins. In response, the youth only smiled. He walked to a nearby fire that was about to be used for a sacrifice and stated coolly, "See how cheap men hold their bodies when they care only for honor."[35] He then thrust his right hand into the flames and held it there, without outcry, as the flesh blackened and sizzled. Utterly astonished, Porsenna ordered his guards to pull Mucius's hand out of the fire. The king admitted that he had never in his life witnessed so much raw courage and suggested that the young man had already suffered enough. Therefore, Porsenna continued, the young man was free to leave and return to his home.

The Fabled Fabii

In addition to the major and in a sense national hero myths that all Romans knew and loved, there were a number of smaller myths of that type that individual Roman families cherished and promoted. They usually dealt with ancestors who had made names for themselves as warriors and patriots five, six, or more generations before. The family continued to worship the memory of those individuals; moreover, now and then a family hero would be adopted by the general public and thereby achieve national status. This was what happened with the noble Fabii family, who over time produced a fair number of noted politicians and other public figures. Back in the 470s BCE, the myth went, Rome was frequently at odds with the Etruscan city of Veii. The Veientes frequently raided Roman farms and quickly retreated before the government could send troops to fight them. In a patriotic gesture, the leaders of the Fabii offered to take care of the Veientes themselves. In a sort of ongoing police action, the clan kept more than three hundred men on immediate call to thwart enemy raids. Eventually, however, the Veientes ambushed and wiped out the Fabii, who were thereafter remembered as fabled heroes of the first order. According to Livy, "Authorities agree that 306 men perished, one only escaping with his life. He was hardly more than a boy, and survived to keep alive the Fabian name and to render high service to Rome in times of need, both in politics and war."

Livy, *The Early History of Rome*, trans. Aubrey de Sélincourt. New York: Penguin, 2002, p. 165.

Mucius then surprised the king again by giving him something in return for his clemency. "Since you respect courage," the young Roman said, "I will tell you in gratitude what you could not force from me by threats."[36] He told Porsenna that there were three hundred other young Roman patriots intent on stopping the siege. One by one, they would gladly give up their lives in order to take that of the Etruscan leader.

After Mucius left Porsenna's camp, the king thought long and hard about what the intrepid young man had said. Would the royal guards be able to detect and deter every one of those enemy assassins? At that moment, based on Horatius's and Mucius's incredible displays of bravery and fortitude, Porsenna reasoned that it might be too costly to conquer Rome. The next day he sent a messenger to tell the Roman leaders he was ready to make peace.

Meanwhile, back in Rome, the young man who had just saved his country was welcomed as a hero. Thereafter, people called him Scaevola—"left-handed"—since that was the only hand that was now of use to him. In a symbolic gesture, in place of his lost right hand the government gave him some farmland on the Tiber's *right* bank.

His Biggest Mistake

According to the myths of early Rome, Scaevola's exploit took place in the late 500s BCE, during the first decade of the fledgling Roman Republic. According to Livy and other later myth tellers, Rome fought numerous battles in the years that followed. The opponents included not only the residents of some nearby Etruscan city-states but also several other neighboring Italian peoples. Of these, among the fiercest were the Volscians, from the hilly lands stretching to the south of the Latium plain.

CORIOLANUS
An early Roman nobleman who turned against his homeland but in the end defended it as a hero

The Volscians posed the biggest threat to Roman territory in the mid-490s BCE. In response to enemy raids on farms in southern Latium, the legend goes, a Roman army assaulted the Volscian stronghold of Corioli. The key Roman general in the siege of that town was Gaius Marcius, believed to be a descendant of one of Rome's kings, Ancus Marcius. Gaius's skill and bravery allowed his countrymen to capture Corioli. To reward him, several high-placed Romans suggested he be given the honorary title of Coriolanus. This was done, and thereafter he was known to history as Gaius Marcius Coriolanus, or Gaius Marcius "of Corioli."

Despite his courage and talents as a military officer, Coriolanus was a nobleman who saw commoners as social inferiors. One day he arrogantly insulted them in public. His attitude "seemed to them excessively harsh," Livy recalled, and "the commons were so infuriated by it that they almost resorted to violence." It was Coriolanus who now felt insulted. As a result, he made his biggest mistake—to abandon his homeland and join up with his former enemies, the Volscians. They "gave him a warm

In this twentieth-century artwork, the arrogant Coriolanus listens to his wife's and mother's pleadings. The mother, Volumnia, urged her son not to turn his back on the nation that had nurtured him. In the end, he followed her advice and for that paid the ultimate price.

Plutarch the Myth Teller

Few ancient writers, including the various tellers of the Greco-Roman myths, ever gained the widespread fame and admiration that Plutarch did. He was born in about 46 CE in the town of Chaeronea, situated several miles north of Athens, Greece. In addition to becoming involved in government affairs in his native city, he became a biographer and moralist, and his notable writing skills gained him a following in both Greek and Roman educated circles. Partly for that reason he made the effort to become a Roman citizen and for a few years actually lived and worked in Rome. Plutarch is most famous for two large-scale literary works. One—the *Parallel Lives*—consists of fifty highly detailed biographies of renowned Greek and Roman military generals, city founders, rulers, and other well-known figures. Among the Romans he covered are Rome's founder, Romulus; the second Roman king, Numa Pompilius; the traitor-turned-hero Coriolanus; and the great military generals Marius and Julius Caesar. Plutarch's second huge literary work—the *Moralia*, or *Moral Essays*—is a collection of absorbing articles on ethical, political, philosophic, scientific, and other issues. Both the biographies and moral essays contain frequent references to Greek and Roman myths, both large and small. Many of the sources Plutarch used for those myths no longer exist; so some of the old tales he tells and details he includes would otherwise be lost to humanity.

welcome," Livy wrote, and "listened to his complaints and threats of revenge against [Rome]."[37]

Soon after Coriolanus joined the Volscians, the Romans held a religious festival to honor Jupiter. The rituals were not performed correctly, which angered that mighty deity. He entered the dream of a leading Roman and warned that the festival must be repeated and in the correct manner, or else he would punish Rome. When the festival restarted, several Volscians showed up to enjoy the festivities, but Roman authorities worried this would further anger Jupiter, so they expelled those foreigners from Rome.

Insulted by this act, the Volscians planned a major attack on Rome and asked Coriolanus himself to lead it. He accepted and guided the Volscian army into Roman territory. Not expecting such an assault, most Romans were distraught. Hundreds of farmers sought refuge behind the city walls, and the temples were filled with people praying to the gods for deliverance.

A Lesson in Loyalty

At this point, the senators picked five of their number to meet with Coriolanus and sue for peace. In Livy's words, he haughtily told them that if all Volscian lands Rome had ever taken "were restored to the Volscians, then peace terms might be discussed."[38] If not, they would attack and take back those lands by force.

The envoys returned to Rome with the bad news that peace might not be obtainable. Most Romans were now extremely worried, but at the last minute a delegation formed to appeal to Coriolanus on personal terms. In the group were his mother, Volumnia, and his wife and children. In the meeting, which took place at the Volscian camp, the women and children suddenly embraced Coriolanus and "burst into tears of anguish for themselves and their country,"[39] Livy said.

This emotional display brought Coriolanus to his senses. He abruptly realized how wrong he had been to turn his back on his country. The divinely inspired heroic qualities within him that had earlier allowed him to defeat the Volscians surfaced once more, and he became determined to save Rome even though he knew it would mean his own death. Wasting no time, he ordered the Volscian troops to retreat and abandon Roman territory. Sure enough, when the Volscian leaders heard what had happened, they arrested and executed Coriolanus.

In later Roman ages, the myth of Coriolanus's sacrifice remained widely popular. People viewed his moving tale as a potent lesson in the importance of showing loyalty to Rome. As had been the case with the Horatii brothers, brave Horatius at the bridge, and Scaevola and his ability to bear pain, Coriolanus also demonstrated that for a Roman, patriotism and love of country must come before all else in life.

CHAPTER FOUR

Women Who Made Rome Great

Women play roles nearly as important as those of men in Roman mythology. The difference between them stems from the fact that Roman society was strongly patriarchal, or subject to the whims and laws of men. As a result, the military generals, rulers, lawmakers, soldier-heroes, and other powerful individuals in society tended to be men. In turn, this was reflected in myths in which men performed various acts of daring and widespread renown.

In contrast, Roman women usually played more subdued roles in society, including those of wife, mother, housekeeper, and in certain special cases priestesses. Yet although their everyday deeds were far less flashy than those of men, women also served as role models, not only for other women but also for all Romans. The virtues and qualities they modeled included both innate morality and strength of character that, when adopted by the citizenry at large, improved the quality of Roman society.

This too was reflected in the myths of early Rome, in which women quietly provide moral and other support behind the scenes for the male fighters and leaders. "For the Romans," Jane F. Gardner points out, mythical women "had the same original purpose as the stories about Rome's male heroes; that is, to encourage acceptance of Roman moral priorities, in particular self-control and self-discipline, in the interests of the Roman state and its security."[40]

A clear example of a mythical woman quietly urging a legendary male leader to exhibit self-control and self-discipline is the case of Volumnia, mother of the haughty hero Coriolanus. Meeting with her son in the Etruscan camp, she reminds him of where his true duties lie and that he was raised to show loyalty to the Roman state above all else. Indeed, it is the influence of Volumnia and another woman, Coriolanus's wife, Virgilia, that shows him how wrong he has been to reject his country and embrace its enemy. Soberly, Volumnia tells him what no man—friend or foe—would think to say. At that moment she is his moral superior and the model patriot he should follow. She lectures him, saying, "When Rome was before your eyes, did not the thought come to you, 'within these walls is my home, with the gods that watch over it, and my mother and my wife, and my children?'"[41]

Porsenna Tries to Save Face

Volumnia and Virgilia were not the only mythical Roman women who were nearly perfect patriots who set examples for their fellow citizens. A few years before the incident with Coriolanus, a young woman named Cloelia became a role model that Roman society was destined to celebrate right down to its final century. When the Etruscan king Lars Porsenna tried to take Rome, he had of course been temporarily impeded when brave Horatius Cocles had engineered the collapse of the only bridge leading across the Tiber. The frustrated but realistic Porsenna realized he would need to wait a while before assaulting Rome again.

For the moment, however, Horatius had made Porsenna look like a failure, and the king felt he needed to try to save face as best he could. One of his advisers quietly pointed out that during the recent Etruscan advance

CLOELIA
A courageous Roman woman who was held hostage by the Etruscans and managed to escape

A seventeenth-century painting shows the heroic Cloelia leading her fellow Romans across the Tiber. According to the Roman historian Livy, Lars Porsenna was at first angry with Cloelia for escaping. But later he declared that she was as great a hero as Horatius.

on Rome, Porsenna's soldiers had managed to seize the Janiculum, a hill that in those days was situated outside the city limits. Thus, although Porsenna did not capture Rome, he did retain control of the Janiculum. Hoping to make it look like he had the upper hand, the king now demanded that Roman leaders give him three dozen hostages. In exchange, he said, he would withdraw his soldiers from the Janiculum.

Death for the Greater Good

Still another mythical young Roman woman whose story was told and retold in later ages was remembered by the name Verginia (or Virginia), meaning "the virgin." Her real name, if she existed at all, remains unknown, so later Romans named her for the chief personal quality she bore in this tale of tyranny and freedom in the Republic's early years. In 451–450 BCE a committee of ten men drew up Rome's first written laws—the Twelve Tables. One of those individuals, named Appius Claudius, fancied himself as a great ruler. With the aid of other powerful men, he seized control of the government and became a ruthless tyrant. He also lusted after an innocent young girl—Verginia, daughter of a Roman general named Verginius. When she refused to have sex with Appius, he took her to court, where, conveniently, he served as the chief judge and there declared her a slave who must do whatever he told her. The father, Verginius, appeared in court to defend her rights, but Appius overruled him. Seeing no other choice, Verginius stabbed his daughter to death, an act she had agreed to in advance, in order to spare her the indignity of slavery and rape. Later, the general overthrew the dictator and restored freedom to all Romans. In this way Verginia joined the ranks of the patriotic women who gave their lives for the greater good of Rome.

The Roman senators did not like the deal Porsenna offered. But they felt they had no choice but to accept because leaving the Janiculum in Etruscan hands was out of the question. The next day, following the senators' command, the three dozen Roman hostages marched in an orderly manner to the Janiculum and surrendered to the Etruscan guards.

To Do Her Duty

Half the prisoners were women, and among them was an unmarried girl named Cloelia. She had consented to follow the senators' order because in her mind obedience and fulfilling the needs of her country were paramount. But those Roman leaders had said nothing about what the hostages should or could do once they were in Etruscan custody. Cloelia reasoned that her country still needed her, and to do her duty and serve it properly, she must first escape. Livy later described the daring plan she enacted, writing, "The Etruscan lines were not far from the Tiber. One day with a number of other girls who had consented to follow her, she eluded the guards, swam across the river under a hail of missiles, and brought her company safe to Rome."[42]

Not surprisingly, the Etruscan king was infuriated that what he scornfully viewed as mere women had made him into a laughing-stock. He forcefully demanded that the Romans return Cloelia immediately. If they did not, he warned, he would consider the deal for the Janiculum to be nullified and would keep the hill. Though proud of Cloelia for her courage, the senators again felt they had no alternative. Thus, they told her to return and give herself up to Porsenna.

When the young woman entered the Etruscan camp a second time, however, she found that the king had had a change of heart. He told her that after his anger had cooled, he had thought about how he would have wanted an Etruscan woman to act under similar circumstances. Clearly, he would desire that she show the bravery and loyalty to her homeland that young Cloelia had shown to her own country. Therefore, he could not be a fair and just ruler if he now punished the young woman for doing what was plainly the right thing.

As a result, Porsenna allowed Cloelia to select a few other hostages and lead them back to Rome. "She is said to have chosen the young boys," according to Livy, "a choice in accordance with her maiden modesty." Furthermore, at least on a temporary basis, "friendly relations were thus restored," and the Etruscans honored the deal and gave up control of the Janiculum. Meanwhile, back in Rome the populace agreed that Cloelia had indeed done her duty to Rome. They "paid tribute to Cloelia's courage, unprecedented in a woman, by an equally unprecedented honor: a statue representing her on horseback."[43]

Sexual Loyalty for the Good of Rome

Among the mythical women who made Rome great, Cloelia stood out as one of the few whose personal chastity was not a major issue in her service to her homeland. Young Roman women, whether mythical or real, were expected to be chaste, or to refrain from having sex before marriage. Yet in the strictest sense a maiden's chief duty was to be virtuous, and in ancient Roman society virtue and chastity were not exactly equivalent. As scholar Elaine Fantham points out, "The Roman woman's primary virtue was *pudicita*, not so much chastity as sexual fidelity enhanced by fertility."[44] That is, a woman should above all commit her life to one man only. Moreover, she should have sex only with him because then her potent fertility will be utilized to produce children strictly for his and her family; in turn, that will strengthen Roman society, itself the sum of many patriotic families working together for the common good of the state.

Regarding this rather complex attribute—*pudicita*, sexual loyalty for the good of Rome—most Roman women upheld this ideal by marrying when young. They then stayed faithful to that one man, had his children, and worked hard within the home and sometimes outside of it to maintain a strong family unit. One such early Roman woman who upheld *pudicita* to the letter was immortalized in a tombstone epitaph by her grief-stricken husband, who wrote, "This tomb, which is not fair, is for a fair woman. Her parents gave her the name Claudia. She loved her husband in her heart. She bore two sons, one of whom she left on earth, the other beneath it. She was pleasant to talk with, and she walked with grace. She kept the home and worked in wool."[45]

Keepers of the Sacred Fire

In both Roman society and Roman mythology, there was a group of young women whose members were by far *both* the most chaste and the most sexually loyal. They were known as the Vestal Virgins, or simply the Vestals for short. In Gardner's words, their "purity was at once the symbol and the guarantee of the welfare of Rome."[46]

The reason it was thought that these special women guarded Rome's well-being was that they were the priestesses and official

The Vestal Virgins attend to Rome's sacred fire. They held considerable social and political influence in Rome. When the first-century dictator Sulla planned to kill the young Julius Caesar, for instance, they intervened and successfully persuaded Sulla to spare Caesar.

keepers of the national hearth, or sacred fire. It was located in the main temple of Vesta, goddess of the hearth. Every Roman home, whether poor or rich, had a hearth, or fireplace, used for cooking and warmth, and the family would gather around it one or more times a day. As the focus of family life, therefore, the hearth was the chief symbol of the Roman family, the most basic unit of society.

The hearth in Vesta's temple, in contrast, was the central symbol of the Roman people, in a sense the national family. It was thought that only if the Vestal priestesses regularly maintained that national fire could the Roman nation prosper and survive into the future. Each Vestal served a minimum of thirty years. During that time, she vowed to be chaste forever. After her service ended, she could marry, but then she had to be sexually loyal as a model for all other Roman women. Any Vestal who broke her vows was punished severely; the penalty was to be buried alive.

The office of the Vestals had formed very early in Rome's dimly remembered past. As a result, the Romans of later centuries maintained several myths about the creation of the state hearth and the exploits of the earliest Vestals. One of those tales involved a Vestal named Aemilia, who was the oldest of the young women then serving in the goddess's temple. One day, the story goes, she allowed a new Vestal to care for the sacred flames on her own, and later in the day the fire died down and went out.

AEMILIA
An early Vestal Virgin who proved she was sexually pure by appealing directly to the goddess Vesta

Rome's male leaders were extremely upset and blamed Aemilia. Had she been secretly unchaste, they wondered, and as a punishment might Vesta have extinguished the fire? When these men questioned Aemilia, who was actually innocent, she stretched out her hands toward the altar and stated emotionally, "O Vesta, guardian of the Romans' city, if, during the space of nearly thirty years, I have performed the sacred offices to you in a holy and proper manner, keeping a pure mind and a chaste body, please manifest yourself in my defense and assist me and do not suffer your priestess to die the most miserable of all deaths."[47] She then tore off a piece of the linen robe she was wearing and threw it onto the altar. Everyone present was startled when a few seconds later the cloth suddenly ignited, producing a bright orange flame that remained strong and bright long after the linen fragment had turned to ashes. With the aid of Vesta herself, all involved agreed, the young woman had proved her innocence.

Ovid the Myth Teller

Publius Ovidius Naso (43 BCE–17 CE), widely known by the shorter nickname Ovid, was one of Augustan Rome's finest writers and leading myth tellers. His lighthearted, often witty and clever writing style made him widely popular both in his own time and in later ages. (He inspired numerous early modern European writers, including the great playwright William Shakespeare.) Ovid's poems were about everyday life, especially themes relating to love and its joys and heartbreaks. One of those related themes was sex, about which Ovid was sometimes quite explicit. The graphic nature of those excerpts irritated the young emperor, Augustus, who was known for being something of a prude. On several occasions he warned the poet to tone himself down, but this advice fell on deaf ears. Finally, having had enough, in 8 CE Augustus exiled Ovid to a small, dreary town on the shores of the Black Sea. There the unhappy author died nine years later. The massive production of writings that survived him include not only poetry but also a large collection of Greco-Roman myths titled the *Metamorphoses*. A noted modern translator of the work, Mary M. Innes, says that Ovid's tellings of those stories reflect the "grace and practiced ease of one who knows well how to hold his audience. The result is a treasure-house of myth and legend which was read with delight in his own day, and has continued to charm succeeding generations, providing a source from which the whole of Western European literature has derived inspiration."

Mary M. Innes, introduction to Ovid, *Metamorphoses*, trans. Mary M. Innes. New York: Penguin, 2006, p. 9.

The Miracle of Claudia Quinta

Vesta was a very ancient Italian fire goddess whom the Romans associated with the Greek deity of the hearth, Hestia. Over time, in addition to older Italian gods and borrowings from the Greek pantheon, the Romans also adopted some other foreign divinities that came to be worshipped across the Roman realm. One of the most popular of those newcomers was Cybele, a wise mother goddess from Anatolia.

The exact manner in which the early Romans found and welcomed Cybele is unclear. So over time a set of myths developed to explain it. One tells about a young Roman woman named Claudia Quinta, who made Cybele's entry into the Roman capital possible. During the final years of the Second Punic War (218–201 BCE), against Carthage, the Romans experienced much death and disruption. Hoping to find a way to alleviate those ills, Roman priests consulted some sacred writings thought to be divinely inspired. The books said that the situation would improve if the Romans welcomed a new deity, specifically Cybele, into their pantheon. Dutifully, therefore, five Roman senators traveled to Anatolia and obtained a sacred black rock thought to represent the goddess. Their ship transported the rock across the sea to western Italy and the mouth of the Tiber River.

There, however, because of a recent drought, the water was shallow, and the boat got stuck in a mass of mud. Hundreds of soldiers and ordinary citizens tugged on ropes, trying to pull the vessel free, but to no avail. Then, out of the crowd stepped young Claudia, who offered to help. Many people ridiculed her because they wrongly suspected that she was unchaste. In any case, some said, how could a single woman succeed where hundreds of strong men had failed? According to Ovid, Claudia ignored the taunts, trudged through the mud, and addressed Cybele's black stone directly, saying, "Kind and fruitful Mother of the Gods, accept a suppliant's prayers."[48]

Then the girl gave a little pull on one of the ropes. To the astonishment of the thousands of onlookers, the huge ship bearing the sacred stone came free from the muck and steadily glided toward her. A few Romans claimed they saw Cybele herself step

In this painting of the female hero Claudia Quinta, painted between 1490 and 1495 by Neroccio de' Landi, the actual scene of her dragging the ship bearing the goddess appears in miniature in the background.

from the vessel and enter the new temple that had been built for her. The promise that she would make the country's fortunes improve was kept, since Rome soon won the war. The Eternal City was saved once more thanks to a lowly but lovingly loyal maiden, one of the many selfless women who helped make Rome great.

CHAPTER FIVE

The Roman Myths in Modern Society

Many of Rome's unique and colorful myths survived the decline and disintegration of the Roman Empire in the 400s and early 500s CE. Later historians also came to label that drawn-out watershed event as the close of ancient times. With that era's end, these very ancient tales passed into the collective folklore, literature, paintings, sculptures, and music of the medieval and early modern European nations and peoples that grew atop the splendid wreckage of the vanished Roman civilization. In turn those societies bequeathed Rome's mythical stories to the modern world. The net result of all this cultural absorption and survival is that today images and themes of mythical Roman gods, founders, heroes, and virtuous women inhabit practically every modern cultural and artistic niche.

These fragmentary recollections of a lost civilization are important not only because they are endlessly entertaining, which no one disputes they are. They are also an integral part of Rome's mighty legacy to later ages. We know who the Romans were partly through scattered ruins of their temples, racetracks, houses, and other structures; we also know them in part from their political writings, laws, and poems that still exist. These tell how they lived and what they did.

But it is no less important to know what the Romans desired from life and what they daydreamed about doing and being—that is, the essence of being Roman. Their myths reveal much of that elusive quality. From those tales we can partially appreciate what the Romans thought of themselves as a people—in a sense the distinctive image that stared back when their collective civilization looked into history's harsh and unforgiving mirror. As Jane F. Gardner puts it, the myths "celebrated the patriotic and moral values cherished, at least as ideals, as being particularly Roman, while often at the same time offering explanations for historical events, or staking a noble family's claim to a prominent place in Rome's tradition. Central, and most important, were the legends about Rome's origins and early growth."[49]

Europe Rediscovers the Old Myths

The survival and transmission of the Roman myths to later peoples did not occur suddenly or even in the same way in various places and times. Instead, for a number of centuries it happened unevenly, in dribs and drabs, with later Europeans rediscovering one or two key Roman myth tellers at a time. The first of those antique writers to gain a major following among intellectuals during the height of the medieval era was Ovid. An upsurge of curiosity about his mythology book, the *Metamorphoses*, spread across Europe's leading cities between about 1000 and 1200.

Driving this trend were priests and other Christian writers who saw in the work's characters and plots a way to teach Christian morality to less educated members of their congregations. Their approach was to compare the diverse pagan mythical characters with individuals in the Bible. In all cases Christian values were depicted as superior to pagan ones. This tactic reached its height in the 1300s with the *Ovide Moralisé*. Composed by an unknown resident of Burgundy, in east-central France, it is a carefully Christianized version of the *Metamorphoses*.

It apparently did not occur to those Christians who manipulated Ovid's work that in the process they were familiarizing new generations of Europeans with the old Roman myths. All through the late medieval centuries, educated Europeans rediscovered the writings of other noted Greco-Roman myth tellers, including Virgil, Livy, Plutarch, and Dionysius of Halicarnassus (late first century BCE). Crucially, all this was happening during the huge outburst of the arts and culture that came to be called the European Renaissance (ca. 1300–1600). As a result, one generation after another of writers and artists of all kinds saw in the Greco-Roman myths rich thematic material.

Literary References to the Myths

Particularly noted among the early modern writers influenced by the Roman myths were dozens of French poets, playwrights, and novelists, including the talented seventeenth-century dramatists Pierre Corneille and Jean Racine. Corneille's tragic play *Horace* (1640), based on Livy's history of Rome, deals with the mythical war between the Romans and Albans in which the Roman Horatii brothers fought their Alban counterparts.

> **PIERRE CORNEILLE**
> A seventeenth-century French dramatist who wrote about the three Horatii brothers

Another French writer of that period who tackled the myths was the seventeenth-century poet Paul Scarron. His *Virgile Travesti*, or "Virgil in Disguise" (1653), is a comic parody of Virgil's epic of the foundation of the Roman race—the *Aeneid*. The poem is humorous partly because Scarron employed some vulgar language. But the comic aspects also derive from purposeful anachronisms (items portrayed in the wrong era). For instance, at one point Scarron has Virgil quote Corneille. Supposedly, when Racine first read the *Virgile Travesti*, he laughed so hard he fell from his chair.

From the 1600s onward English writers also produced a considerable amount of literature based on the Roman myths. Most famous among these works were those of the great sixteenth-century playwright William Shakespeare. Whole volumes have

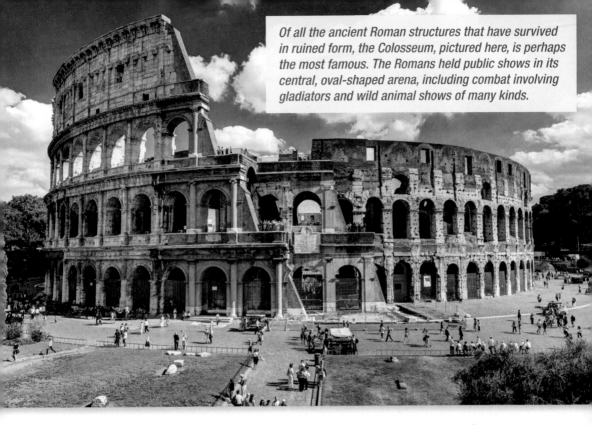

Of all the ancient Roman structures that have survived in ruined form, the Colosseum, pictured here, is perhaps the most famous. The Romans held public shows in its central, oval-shaped arena, including combat involving gladiators and wild animal shows of many kinds.

been composed detailing his hundreds of references to characters and situations from Greco-Roman mythology. Most of the material for those references came from the writings of Plutarch, Livy, Virgil, and Ovid.

In addition to his many individual allusions to characters and events from the Roman myths, Shakespeare wrote an entire play about the mythical Roman traitor-turned-hero Coriolanus. Dating from sometime in the playwright's late writing period (likely between 1605 and 1608), it mainly utilizes Plutarch's biography of Coriolanus for plot and characters. Though one of the least performed of Shakespeare's plays today, it is arguably one of his best. He was attracted to the story, former York University scholar Beryl Rowland explains,

> because of its dramatic possibilities. The hero was a paradox, a man of uncompromising integrity, lacking, it would seem, both the tender qualities and the petty failings of lesser men, yet becoming a traitor and then, in

turn, betraying his new allies because of the warmth of family ties. Here was a new challenge of a difficult kind and it could be worked out in scenes of tremendous theatrical potential. . . . Even reading the play one knows it must be good theater.[50]

A later noted English writer also saw the inherent dramatic qualities in the myths about early Roman heroes. In a lengthy 1842 ode of seventy densely written stanzas, historian, politician, and poet Thomas Babington Macaulay described the courage and superior swordplay of the title character of *Horatius at the Bridge*. The work was immensely popular in the mid- to late nineteenth century, and English schoolchildren routinely recited passages from it. Also, heroic lines from Macaulay's *Horatius* were later quoted in popular science fiction TV shows ranging from *Star Trek* to *Dr. Who*.

The Roman Myths Inspire Artists

Roman mythology also became major source material for painters, sculptors, printmakers, and other Renaissance and early modern artists. For example, a painting on an Italian dish made in about 1544 shows Volumnia lecturing her son, Coriolanus, in the Etruscan camp. A century later Italian artist Giovanni Francesco Barbieri, better known as Guercino, depicted the same subject in his painting *Volumnia Before Coriolanus*. A still later painted version of that same scene is *Volumnia Pleading with Coriolanus*, by England's Richard Westall.

The stories of Rome's founders—Aeneas and his descendants Romulus and Remus—inspired various artists as well. Aeneas's myth proved particularly popular, and *Aeneas Fleeing the Burning Troy* became the title of countless paintings created by Europeans. One of the finest is a work by sixteenth-century Italian Federico Barocci. Romulus and Remus were the subjects of a major painting in the following century by the great Belgian artist Peter

The great Belgian painter Peter Paul Rubens produced this atmospheric rendering of the shepherd Faustulus finding the infants Romulus and Remus being fed by a she-wolf. According to legend, when the boys grew up Remus died and Romulus went on to found Rome alone.

Paul Rubens. It shows the shepherd Faustulus finding the young twins being fed by a female wolf.

Another legendary Roman hero—Horatius Cocles—was captured by numerous artists from the 1400s on. One is a black-and-white engraving of that warrior striding along in full armor. Created by seventeenth-century Dutch printmaker Hendrick Goltzius, it is still used today in books and online articles that mention the character. Also popular is *Horatius Cocles Defending the Bridge*, a magnificent oil on canvas by the seventeenth-century French painter Charles Le Brun. Showing a Roman goddess floating above the hero and guiding his hands, it hangs today in one of Europe's premiere art museums, London's Dulwich Picture Gallery.

The famous mythical Roman women have also been favorite subjects for artists. One, depicting the maiden Claudia Quinta pulling the Roman ship from the mud, was created by the late

David's Great Myth-Based Paintings

Few Renaissance, early modern, or modern painters were as inspired by the characters and stories of Roman mythology as France's Jacques-Louis David. Born on August 30, 1748, in Paris, he was only nine when his father died in a duel. The grief-stricken mother then left the boy to be raised by two uncles. These men fortunately recognized early that the child had artistic gifts and sent him to a family friend who was also a professional painter, François Boucher. The latter soon saw that young Jacques-Louis was not simply talented but possibly potentially a world-class artist, and the young man eventually ended up at France's Royal Academy of Painting and Sculpture. After graduating, he fulfilled his great potential and produced some of history's finest paintings, including several depicting famous episodes from Roman mythology. One, *The Oath of the Horatii*, completed in 1784, shows the three Roman brothers standing before their father, grasping their swords and swearing to fight to the death for Rome against the Albans. Another myth-inspired canvas—*The Lictors Bring Brutus the Bodies of His Sons* (1789)—captures a key moment from the formation of the Roman Republic, and *The Intervention of the Sabine Women* (1799) shows those women thrusting their bodies between the Roman and Sabine armies in an attempt to stop a bloodbath.

Renaissance Belgian painter Lambert Lombard. In the early eighteenth century, Italy's Alessandro Marchesini painted *Dedication of a New Vestal Virgin*; it shows a new Vestal being welcomed into Vesta's temple as several legendary Vestals of the past float in the smoke rising from the sacred fire.

Interestingly, the myths about the Vestals and other chaste Roman women became so popular in Europe in the 1700s that they spawned a new fad. Wealthy women in France, Germany, and other neighboring countries spent considerable sums to commission painters to portray them as Vestal Virgins. One of the many surviving examples is *Portrait of a Woman as a Vestal Virgin*, by eighteenth-century female Swiss artist Angelica Kauffman.

Music and Movies

Music is another artistic venue that has been inspired by the characters, events, and ideas of the Roman myths. One of the first early modern composers to utilize those old stories was seventeenth-century English musician Henry Purcell. His 1689 opera, *Dido and Aeneas*, concentrates on the doomed relationship between the wandering Trojan hero Aeneas and Dido, queen of Carthage. Realizing that the man she loves will not return to her from Italy, Dido sings a song in which she urges him to do his best to forget about her. Then she commits suicide. The work deals with the connection of the two characters from her point of view, whereas the more recent opera *Aeneas and Dido* (2007), by Canadian composer James Rolfe, concentrates more on Aeneas's inner feelings and motivations.

By far the largest-scale and most famous musical excursion into the Roman myths is the opera *Les Troyens*, or "The Trojans" (1858), by the great French composer Hector Berlioz. He based the work directly on Virgil's *Aeneid*. Due to its length—almost five hours—it is usually staged in two parts—*The Fall of Troy* and *The Trojans at Carthage*—on successive nights.

HECTOR BERLIOZ
The great nineteenth-century French composer of *Les Troyens*, an opera about Aeneas's adventures

There have also been dramatic films of Aeneas's Roman foundation tale. The one produced in Italy in 1962—*The Last Glory of Troy*—was low budget and made many unnecessary changes to Virgil's story. Much more faithful to the original material, as well as better made, was an ambitious Italian television miniseries appropriately titled *Aeneid* (1971). Lavishly mounted, it starred the handsome and popular Italian actor Giulio Brogi as Aeneas.

The other major Roman foundation myth—in which Romulus establishes the eternal city—has also made it to movie screens more than once. The most colorful version was *Duel of the Titans*

This mid-nineteenth-century poster advertises a performance of French composer Hector Berlioz's splendid opera The Trojans. *It is rarely produced today, mainly because its spectacular sets and numerous actor-singers and extras require a huge budget.*

(1961), with famed bodybuilder Steve Reeves as Romulus. Despite Reeves's wooden acting, the film remains mostly true to its source material—Plutarch's *Life of Romulus* and Livy's massive history of Rome. In his book about filmed versions of ancient peoples, University of Arizona scholar Jon Solomon writes, "The look of the film is enhanced by expansive crane shots of the beautiful wooded [hills] not far from where the events of the ancient stories were supposed to have taken place in 753 BCE." Also, Solomon credits the production's use of sets and costumes that are fitting for the era and places portrayed. This evocative atmosphere, he says, "elevates the film above most other sword-and-sandal movies of its day."[51]

Arguably the best movie version of a Roman myth made to date was the British production of a modern-day version of *Coriolanus* released in 2011. Starring and directed by popular actor Ralph Fiennes, the film is thoughtfully staged and well-acted. Andrew Pulver, a film critic for the *Guardian*, wrote, "The great strength of Fiennes's

Dionysius the Myth Teller

Dionysius of Halicarnassus was a Greek historian who was born in that major city in Anatolia in about 60 BCE. His first few decades therefore spanned the destructive civil wars that brought down the Roman Republic. Shortly after Octavian won the last of those conflicts in 31 BCE, Dionysius moved to Rome and there spent some twenty years studying Latin and Roman history. During that time he got to know a number of Roman scholars, as well as at least one of Octavian's Greek tutors. So it is possible that Dionysius met the future Augustus at some point. What is more certain is that sometime during Augustus's reign, the Greek historian published his masterpiece, the *Roman Antiquities*. It covers Rome's mythical period, beginning a bit before the advent of Romulus, and concludes at the beginning of the First Punic War in the 260s BCE. Of the work's twenty books, or sections, nine have survived complete, two are nearly complete, and the rest exist in fragments or summaries in the works of other ancient writers. The *Roman Antiquities* contains numerous references to traditional Roman myths and has an especially detailed account of the Roman foundation myth involving Romulus and Remus. In fact, both Livy and Plutarch relied heavily on Dionysius's account in writing their own versions of Romulus's exploits. The date of Dionysius's death is unknown, but some evidence suggests it was well before the end of Augustus's reign, in 14 CE.

film is simply its clarity and intelligence. He's clearly paid a great deal of detailed attention to how the narrative and the interplay of character is to work—vital in Shakespeare films."[52]

Part of the Fabric of Modern Life

These few dozen examples of how the Roman myths have been revitalized in modern arts and culture barely scratch the surface of the world's inheritance of those ancient stories. Their characters and themes, the late, prolific historian Michael Grant observed, are intimately interwoven "with the whole fabric of [our] public and private lives." Without these myths, he added, "we should be hard put to understand the arts and literature and ways of thinking of the West [during] the centuries that have passed since the [ancient] world came to an end." Time and again, Grant wrote, those old expressions of the ancient imagination have inspired fresh creative uses. These range from poetry and plays to paintings and films. Indeed, Grant noted, so great has been the cultural contribution of these vintage tales to later ages that "the revitalizing of the classical myths can be claimed as the most significant of all the impacts that the Greco-Roman world has made upon modern thought."[53]

SOURCE NOTES

Introduction: Blurring the Boundary Between Legend and Reality

1. Livy, *The Early History of Rome*, trans. Aubrey de Sélincourt. New York: Penguin, 2002, p. 115.
2. Livy, *The Early History of Rome*, p. 116.
3. Jane F. Gardner, *Roman Myths*. Austin: University of Texas Press, 1993, p. 10.
4. Gardner, *Roman Myths*, p. 9.
5. Quoted in Virgil, *Aeneid*, trans. Patric Dickinson. New York: New American Library, 2002, pp. 10–11.
6. Donald L. Wasson, "Roman Mythology," Ancient History Encyclopedia, May 8, 2018. www.ancient.eu.

Chapter One: The Ancient Romans and Their Gods

7. Virgil, *Aeneid*, p. 4.
8. R.M. Ogilvie, *The Romans and Their Gods in the Age of Augustus*. New York: Norton, 1969, p. 11.
9. Gardner, *Roman Myths*, p. 13.
10. Ogilvie, *The Romans and Their Gods in the Age of Augustus*, p. 4.
11. Gardner, *Roman Myths*, p. 78.
12. Ovid, *Metamorphoses*, trans. Mary M. Innes. New York: Penguin, 2006, p. 357.
13. Virgil, *Aeneid*, p. 173.

Chapter Two: Rome's Primary Foundation Myths

14. Virgil. *Aeneid,* p. 27.
15. Gardner, *Roman Myths*, p. 16.
16. T.J. Cornell, *The Beginnings of Rome: Italy and Rome from the Bronze Age to the Punic Wars*. London: Routledge, 1995, p. 65.

17. Virgil, *Aeneid*, p. 30.
18. Virgil, *Aeneid*, p. 67.
19. Virgil, *Aeneid*, pp. 172–73.
20. Norma L. Goodrich, *Ancient Myths*. New York: Plume, 1994, p. 250.
21. Virgil, *Aeneid*, p. 11.
22. Plutarch, *Romulus*, trans. John Dryden, Internet Classics Archive. http://classics.mit.edu.
23. Livy, *Livy: The Early History of Rome*, p. 29.
24. Plutarch, *Romulus*.
25. Livy, *Livy: The Early History of Rome*, pp. 42–43.
26. Ovid, *Fasti*, trans. A.J. Boyle and R.D. Woodward, Theoi Greek Mythology. www.theoi.com.
27. Plutarch, *Romulus*.
28. Cornell, *The Beginnings of Rome*, p. 60.

Chapter Three: The Warrior Heroes of Early Rome

29. Gardner, *Roman Myths*, p. 41.
30. Livy, *Livy: The Early History of Rome*, pp. 57–58.
31. Livy, *Livy: The Early History of Rome*, p. 60.
32. Livy, *Livy: The Early History of Rome*, p. 118.
33. Livy, *Livy: The Early History of Rome*, p. 118.
34. Livy, *Livy: The Early History of Rome*, pp. 118–19.
35. Livy, *Livy: The Early History of Rome*, p. 119.
36. Livy, *Livy: The Early History of Rome*, p. 119.
37. Livy, *Livy: The Early History of Rome*, p. 145.
38. Livy, *Livy: The Early History of Rome*, p. 149.
39. Livy, *Livy: The Early History of Rome*, p. 150.

Chapter Four: Women Who Made Rome Great

40. Gardner, *Roman Myths*, p. 53.
41. Quoted in Livy, *Livy: The Early History of Rome*, p. 150.
42. Livy, *Livy: The Early History of Rome*, p. 120.
43. Livy, *Livy: The Early History of Rome*, p. 120.
44. Elaine Fantham, "Republican Rome I," in Elaine Fantham et al, eds., *Women in the Classical World*. New York: Oxford University Press, 1994, p. 225.

45. Quoted in Eva Cantarella, *Pandora's Daughters: The Role and Status of Women in Greek and Roman Antiquity*. Baltimore: Johns Hopkins University Press, 1987, p. 133.
46. Gardner, *Roman Myths*, p. 55.
47. Quoted in Dionysius of Halicarnassus, *Roman Antiquities*, trans. Earnest Cary, Bill Thayer's Website, February 18, 2012. http://penelope.uchicago.edu.
48. Ovid, *Fasti, Book 4*, trans. A.S. Kline, Poetry in Translation. www.poetryintranslation.com.

Chapter Five: The Roman Myths in Modern Society
49. Gardner, *Roman Myths*, p. 78.
50. Beryl Rowland, "Introduction to *Coriolanus*," in *Coriolanus*, by William Shakespeare. New York: Airmont, 1968, pp. xviii–xix.
51. Jon Solomon, *The Ancient World in the Cinema*. New Haven, CT: Yale University Press, 2001, pp. 129–30.
52. Andrew Pulver, "Coriolanus: Review," *Guardian* (Manchester), February 15, 2011. www.theguardian.com.
53. Michael Grant, *Myths of the Greeks and Romans*. New York: Plume, 1995, pp. xvii, xix.

FOR FURTHER RESEARCH

Books

Anthony Augoustakis, *Epic Heroes on Screen*. Edinburgh: Edinburgh University Press, 2019.

Jane Bingham, *Classical Myth: A Treasury of Greek and Roman Legends, Art, and History*. London: Routledge, 2016.

Matt Clayton, *Roman Mythology*. Scotts Valley, CA: CreateSpace, 2018.

David E. Falkner, *The Mythology of the Night Sky: An Amateur Astronomer's Guide to the Ancient Greek and Roman Legends*. New York: Springer, 2011.

William Hansen, *The Book of Greek and Roman Folktales, Legends, and Myths*. Princeton, NJ: Princeton University Press, 2019.

Sarah I. Johnston, *The Story of Myth*. Cambridge, MA: Harvard University Press, 2018.

David Stuttard, *Roman Mythology: A Traveler's Guide from Troy to Tivoli*. London: Thames and Hudson, 2019.

Internet Sources

Saugat Adhicari, "Top 10 Popular and Fascinating Myths in Ancient Rome," July 12, 2019. www.ancienthistorylists.com.

Charles Morris, "The Story of Lucretia," Gateway to the Classics. www.mainlesson.com.

Vera Norman, "Four Conceptions of the Heroic," Fellowship of Reason. www.fellowshipofreason.com/archives/4heroes.htm.

Plutarch, *Romulus*, trans. John Dryden, Internet Classics Archive. http://classics.mit.edu.

UNRV, "Publius Ovidius Naso (Ovid)," 2019. www.unrv.com.

Donald L. Wasson, "Roman Mythology," Ancient History Encyclopedia, May 8, 2018. www.ancient.eu.

Websites

Encyclopedia of Greek Mythology, Mythweb (www.mythweb.com/encyc). This website provides a lot of useful information about both major and minor Greek mythological characters. Roman equivalents are noted where appropriate.

Theoi Greek Mythology (www.theoi.com). This is the most comprehensive and reliable general website about Greek mythology on the internet. It features hundreds of separate pages filled with detailed, accurate information, as well as numerous primary sources and reproductions of ancient paintings and mosaics. Roman equivalents are noted where appropriate.

Virgil's _Aeneid_, Classics Pages (www.users.globalnet.co.uk/~loxias/aeneid1.htm). A simplified translation of book 1 of Virgil's classic tale of Aeneas and the founding of the Roman race.

INDEX

PICTURE CREDITS

ABOUT THE AUTHOR

Classical historian and award-winning author Don Nardo has written numerous acclaimed volumes about ancient civilizations and peoples. They include more than a dozen overviews of the mythologies of the Sumerians, Babylonians, Egyptians, Greeks, Romans, Persians, Celts, and others. Nardo, who also composes and arranges orchestral music, lives with his wife, Christine, in Massachusetts.